Right to The Heart

Author: Willeen G. Williams

Right to the heart

Right to The Heart

Author: Willeen G. Williams

Right to the heart

The Alpha Word House Publisher

Copyright ©2017 by Willeen G. Williams

Library of Congress Cataloging in
Publication Data

Washington, D.C.

Right to The Heart

Author: Willeen G. Williams

ISBN - 978-0-9987241-5-7

Printed in the United States of American.

Right to the Heart

Author: Willeen G. Williams

Right to the heart

Contents

Right to the heart

Right to the heart

Right to the heart

Right to the heart

Right to the heart

Right to the heart

Right to the heart

Splendor is our King

Splendor is our King Jesus.

Praises and worship unto Jesus Holy Name.

Love, and we adore you forever more.

Everlasting King the joy you bring.

Now powerful and great is our king.

Rejoicing in the splendor of our King.

In God's Glory filled with love precious
King from above.

Say, yes to our King, and rejoice in Jesus
Holy Name.

My heart is rejoicing, oh King of king.

Yes, praise the Mighty King for the love he
brings.

Keep praising our King, and let all the earth
rejoice.

In my heart, it is filled with love from the

Master up above. Now, let us rejoice, let

rejoice, rejoice, rejoice. Great is our King a

Chief ruler over everything.

Right to the heart

Never give in

Never give up.

Even, never show a frown.

Victory is in Jesus.

Every time you are feeling down.

Rest in the arms of Jesus.

Great almighty is our King.

In Jesus name, there is peace.

Victory you will gain in Jesus name.

Even during your tears.

Ups and downs.

Praise the name of Jesus, you will always be

a winner.

Right to the heart

Keeping Jesus

Keeping your faith.

keeping your dreams.

keeping your hope.

keeping your love.

keeping your peace.

keeping your joy.

keeping the love of Jesus in your heart fore

ever more.

Right to the heart

God is great

God is great.

God is always good.

God is blessing you.

God is keeping you.

God is watching you.

God is awakening you.

God will never forsake you.

God is sure enough great to you.

Right to the heart

It is never too late

It is never too late to dream.

It is never too late to try.

It is never too late when waiting .

It is never too late to go forth.

It is never too late to walk in your destiny.

Just remember Jesus is always standing bye.

Right to the heart

People

People are filled with love.

Every touch from the hands above.

On this earth people make mistakes.

People sometimes laugh and cry.

Listening and waiting for a touch from the

Master's hands.

Every day Jesus is standing bye when you
cry.

Now, the tears are gone, and Jesus you can

depend on.

Right to the heart

Look unto Jesus

Look unto Jesus.

Look unto Jesus because he will make away.

Look unto Jesus, the mighty author, finisher of your faith.

Look unto Jesus, and he will show you a brighter day.

Look unto Jesus, and he will turn your midnight into day.

Look unto Jesus, and he will guide you every step of the way.

Right to the heart

Help is on the way

Help is all you need.

Even when you are going through.

Looking unto Jesus.

Please, Jesus don't pass me bye.

During my storm.

Still holding on to my Master's hands.

In the misty dawn.

Never will I let go, and now safe am I in the

Master's arms.

The day may have seemed a little tough.

Help was on the way even before dawn.

Even in the storm, you kept holding on.

Wipe the tears from your eyes, victory is

won. It is time go to bed, and no tears you

need to shed. You keep the faith, and don't

you worry. Jesus will be there for you

always in a hurry.

Right to the heart

A cry in the dark

Oh, a silent cry in the dark.

There is a suddenly outburst of pain.

My heart feels your struggles.

It is like you walking in the rain.

There is no shelter to cover your head

Jesus is always there to protect you no

matter what anyone says, and that's ok.

Right to the heart

Hold On

Help is on the way.

Oh, don't let your hands slip away.

Never give up not one day.

Don't give up today.

Oh, your help is on the way.

Never give up.

Never look down.

Hold on to your smile

Jesus will be there to turn your whole life

around.

Right to the heart

Remember Jesus is Love

Remember Jesus is love.

Everlasting and full of Joy.

Master of your ship.

Every pounding wave in the ocean.

Merciful, and kind King Jesus is to me.

Bright as the sun that sat in the sky.

Every star Jesus hung up in the sky.

Remember Jesus done it all for you, and I.

Right to the heart

My Age

At the age of one sitting on mommy knee.

At the age of two, I like to play pee a boo.

At the age of three, I like to sit by the tree.

At the age of four, I love to explore.

At the age of five, I got on the slide.

At the age of six, I can pick up a stick.

At the age of seven, thought I was cleaver.

At the age of eight, I stood by the gate.

At the age of nine, I saw a big sign.

At the age of ten, I am still growing again.

Right to the heart

Places

Places can be large or small.

Looking high or low.

All around you in the earth there is beauty.

Calm, and a gentle breeze just pass by me.

Even walking on the beach sand on my feet.

Sun, set is so high in the sky a beautiful

place that caught my eye.

Right to the heart

Giving God your time

Giving me your time to listen

Even during your busy day.

Viewing over the things you need to do.

Making no excuse to stop along the way.

Every day is not the same.

You keep going on it is not a game.

Oh, just keep your praises up in Jesus name.

Ups and down in life may flow.

Reach up, and press for Jesus even the more.

Take your time, and don't resign.

In the storm God will deliver you just in time.

My God is big enough to see you through.

Everlasting God, a Prince of Peace came and rescue me.

Right to the heart

My Heart

My heart it searches for peace.

My heart it searches for love.

My heart searches for joy.

My heart it searches happiness.

My heart it felt the touch from up above.

That is a touch of the Master called love.

Right to the heart

The hand print on Calvary Cross

The hand print on Calvary Cross.

The hand that saved our souls from sin.

The hand print to save us from being lost.

The hand print that died to set us free.

The hand print died to save a soul like me.

The hand print that died on the cross.

The hand print dropped his head, and died.

The mother of Jesus cried, and wiping the

tears from her eyes.

Jesus never said one word he just hung his

and died

The hand print that died on Calvary Cross.

Right to the heart

Moon Light

Today is a beautiful night.

Happy as I can be.

Every day the moon is shining right at me.

Morning has now appeared.

Oh, listen to the birds singing my dear.

Oh, listening to the wind blowing in my ear.

Night is soon coming my dear.

Lights are shining up and down the street.

I looked up at the beautiful sky.

Gleam is shining in my eyes.

Happy, happy, happy, am I.

There is a big twinkle in the sky.

Right to the heart

Praising God

Raising up early in the morning.

A praise is always on my lips.

I love to rejoice in the Lord.

Sound of sweet praise in my ear.

I hear the praises going up.

Never will I stop.

Great is the King.

God of the whole universe.

Oh, how wonderful is King Jesus name.

Day by day, I will praise King Jesus name.

Right to the heart

The sound of a train

The sound of a train.

Hearing the whistle blow.

Every wheel turning some more.

Tracks are all holding tight.

Racing down the tracks day, and night.

All the rumbling sound of the train.

I hear the train even across town.

Noisy sound all around.

Oh, the train is still passing through.

Now, you know what to do.

Take all the caution, and let the train go too.

Happy to see the train passing through.

Everyone is waiting for the train to go away.

The train caboose is holding on tight.

Right at the track, I see red flashing lights.

All a board on this train.

Choo, choo, right down the track again
tonight.

Right to the heart

You are loved

You are loved.

Open your eyes.

Open your heart to another day.

Rest in the arms of Jesus right away.

Always standing by your side.

Ready to keep you from all your fears.

Every day keep Jesus on your mind.

Loving Jesus is the best of times.

Open your heart let Jesus come in.

Victory in Christ, and will give it unto thee.

Every living day you will awake to victory.

Day by day Jesus love is guaranteed to stay.

Right to the heart

Thank you, papa

Thank you, papa.

Helping me.

All the time.

Never leaving me alone.

Keeping me safe in the home.

You are a blessing to me.

Oh, how happy I can be.

Up and down on the merry go around.

Please don't let me hit the ground.

All around and around.

Please don't let me fall on the ground.

All around and around

Thank you, papa.

Right to the heart

Red Roses

Red roses are beautiful.

Early in the morning, my dear.

During anytime of the day.

Red roses are still looking fine.

Oh, still beautiful even when the sun shines.

Showers of rain will make it grow.

Every beautiful red rose stands by my door.

Right to the heart

Tick, Tick, Tock

Tick, tick, tock.

I hear the clock.

Clock struck one.

Keep moving on.

Tick, tick, tock.

I hear the clock.

Clock struck two.

Keep moving on.

Tick, tick, tock.

Oh, it will not stop.

Clock struck three.

Keep on moving you are free.

Right to the heart

Grand mom in the kitchen

Grand mom in the kitchen.

Grand mom in the kitchen baking bread.

Grand mom in the kitchen cooking grits.

Grand mom in the kitchen cooking bacon.

Grand mom in the kitchen cooking eggs.

Grand mom in the kitchen setting the table.

Grand mom in the kitchen, wash your hands.

Grand mom in the kitchen, time to pray, and
eat again.

Right to the heart

Playing with my blocks

Playing with my blocks.

I am just a little tot.

Playing with my blocks.

One, two, three.

Playing with my blocks.

I am just a little tot.

Building a car with my blocks.

Playing with my blocks

I enjoy being a little tot.

Right to the heart

Lady in blue

Lady in blue.

Already to walk through.

Down the street I can see you.

You are smiling all over town.

In the middle of the day you say hey.

Never will you give up any way.

Brave and singing a song.

Up and down town, I am gone.

Every day waiting for the lady in blue.

Right to the heart

Stars

Stars are shinning

Stars are bright

Stars are shinning to night

Stars are in my sight

Stars are beautiful tonight.

Right to the heart

Walking in the park

Walking in the park

Oh, wow it is not even dark

Walking in the park

All around the park we go

Looking to see a lot more

Keeping my eyes opened wide

In the park a lot of rides

Grand pa even went inside.

I enjoyed seeing the park again

Now the park is beautiful within

There are so much amusements and rides

Happy to see the children even on the slides

Even see the twinkles in their eyes

Pressing my way through the crowd

All the happy, smiles

Resting along the way

Keeping a smile on my face to stay.

Right to the heart

Dreams

Dreams are dreams.

Ready to see what it means.

Every dream is in the night.

All the dreams you have hold on tight.

Memories of all my dreams, and your eyes

are still bright.

Right to the heart

The heart beats

The heart beats in the middle of the night

Heavenly father keeps the heart beats right

Every time it may seem to flutter

Hands of God is powerful and better

Even the stroke of a pen God always wins

After all, God has all the power in his hands

Rest assure Jesus is always on time

Trust in God, and never doubt

Believe always God will bring you out

Ever tear that flow from your eyes Jesus is

still standing bye

All your tears, Jesus will wipe away.

The pain, tears, sleepless nights, and God

able to keep your heart beat flowing right.

Right to the heart

Just in time

Just in time

Uphill journey you are going through

Stay safe with God, and you are just in time

Trust his love, God has for you

In God's arms you will feel protected

Never will you ever be disconnected

Trust in Jesus every time for a peaceful
mind.

In the time of trouble God will always keep
you.

My heart is rejoicing, and I found Jesus just
in time.

Every praise, I will give unto my God

Forever, and forever mines.

Right to the heart

Fishing

Fishing is a pleasure.

Even in the hottest weather.

Sitting here on the pier.

Waiting for a bite to appear.

Happy as I can be 1, 2, 3.

The fish is caught on the hook by me.

Right to the heart

Nothing too hard for God

Nothing too hard for God.

Oh, wait on God to see you through

Trust God to do it for you

Help is on the way today

In the middle of your struggles

Nothing too hard for God to do

Great is your faithfulness to God

Trusting in God will do it for you

Oh, I know God will see me through

Hold on don't let go of Jesus hands

Always trusting God to the being to the end

Rest in God's arms night and day

Don't you ever doubt, no way

Forever trusting God every step of the way

Oh, just wait until God bring you out

Rest in God's arms don't you faint

God is great, and God is always good

Never doubt God be there for you.

Right to the heart

Keep Pressing

Pressing is the thing to do

Resting is the thing I need to do

Eating is what I need to do

Sleeping is the thing to do

In a quiet place

Now, I can rest in this place too

Getting the rest, I need is important

Yes, this a beautiful day

Oh, mine how sometimes time fly way

Underneath the stars the lighted sky

Resting again my sleepy eyes

Watching and waiting to see day break.

Already to press my way today

Yes, it is another great day to keep pressing.

Right to the heart

Stay anchor in Jesus

Stay anchor in Jesus

Turn not away from God ever

You keep holding on day and night

Alright never let go of Jesus

Nail scarred hands of a mighty man, Jesus

Came to free man from sins, Jesus

Hanged on the cross at all cost

Oh, our souls will not be lost

Righteous is King Jesus

In Jesus arms I always feel protected

Never will I feel neglected

Jesus will hold my hands even until the end

Every day with Jesus is sweeter and sweeter

Stay anchor in Jesus

Unto the Masters hands

Stay aboard, and never give up on the Lord.

Right to the heart

Worthy

Worthy is the lamb

Oh, whom have die on Calvary Cross

Rest, Jesus had paid the price for you, and I.

Trusting in Jesus Holy name.

Happy that Jesus has spared us again.

Yes, Jesus is worthy to be praise.

Right to the heart

Thankful

Thankful is me

Happy as I can be

All day and night

Now can't you see

Keep being thankful

For all the good things

Unto Jesus is the same

Thankful to be free.

Right to the heart

Whisper

Whisper in the day

Hearing a gentle breeze

In middle of the day break

Sounds of the brushing leaves

Picking up the beautiful sounds of the wind

Evening is still a breeze

Relaxing and hearing the whisper sounds

again.

The tranquility of my mind flowed freely.

Right to the heart

Praise

Praise will release a blessing

Reaching upward to the sky

Almighty is the King standing bye

I feel the praises of the King

Sweet sounding joy the Master will bring

Every twinkle in your eye Jesus is near bye.

Right to the heart

Never give up

Never give up

Everything feels like it is going down

Victory is all around

Ever sound of trouble

Rest, God is giving you double for your

trouble.

Right to the heart

My mind

My mind is free

Yes, in the middle of a trouble world

Making my mind to relax

In the middle of the day

Now, you smile and say hey

Day has now past my mind is free at last.

Right to the heart

Go ahead

Go ahead start your day

Looking ahead beautiful month of May

Alright the sun is shining bright

Down the path is a beautiful bright light.

Right to the heart

Let it go

Let it go

Even during the pressures of life

Try to get you down

It is important to hold your head up

Trust in the Master up above

God goodness and mercy filled with love

Open arms, Jesus love is still growing

strong.

.

Right to the heart

Packing up

Packing up

All the way around

Checking and looking

Keeping a. solid smile

In the middle of the crowd

Never showing any fear

Going around to see who is here

Up, now the time is far spent

Packing up now for the next event.

Right to the heart

Apples

Apples, apples, apples

Apples tastes mighty fine

Apples, apples, apples

Apples picked from a tree

Apples, apples, apples

Apples are red

Apples, apples, apples

Apples are green

Apples, apples, apples

I do agree

Apples are mighty good to me.

Right to the heart

Two Birds in a tree

Two birds sitting in a tree

One bird name Red, and one is Blue

Two birds sitting in a tree

Red bird said good morning to you in the

tree.

Two birds sitting in a tree

Blue said good morning indeed

Two birds sitting in a tree

Red bird is singing happy as I can be

Two birds sitting up in a tree

Blue bird is singing can't you see

Two birds sitting in a tree

Red bird been singing, since he was three

Two birds sitting in a tree

Blue bird been singing since he was three

Two birds now sitting in a tree

Now, it is only you, and me.

Right to the heart

Biking

Biking is fun to do

In the park I love to ride through

Keeping my pace throughout the day

I love to bike ride in the park with you

Now people are riding bikes in town too

Great day to ride my bike in the park, and all

around town.

Right to the heart

Red Rooster

Red rooster, red rooster

Crowing before it is dawn

Red rooster, red rooster

Now, it is time to start your day on

Red roster is raised on a farm

Red rooster is kept in a barn.

Right to the heart

Protection

Protection is a need indeed

Reaching for more love from above

On this journey to find true love

Taking nothing for granted

Each day of my life

Choosing Jesus first in my life

Take care of me through the thick and thin

I will always feel God's protection

Oh, I never once felt disconnected

Now, I am blessed and protected.

Right to the heart

Bridges

Bridges cross many things in life

Bridge cross over the rivers

Oh, we will cross that bridge you see

Bridges are beautiful to see

There are bridges bigger than you and me

There are even over path bridges to take us

where we need to go.

Jesus is the bridge over trouble water, and

forever more.

Right to the heart

Wise Owl

Wise owl is sitting up in a tree

Wise owl is looking down at me

Wise owl is sitting up in a tree

Wise owl goes hoo-ah, hoo

Wise owl sitting up in a tree

Wise owl sitting, and his eyes big and looking at me.

Wise owl said hoo-ah, hoo

Wise owl sitting up in a tree

Wise owl is fat as can be

Wise owl goes hoo-ah, hoo

Wise owl sitting up in a tree.

Right to the heart

Patty Cake

Patty cake Patty cake

Mommy, I know you can

Patty cake, patty cake

Mommy, please mix it, know you can

Patty cake, patty cake

Mommy, please put in a pan

Patty cake, patty cake

Mommy, now bake it in the oven

Patty cake, patty cake

Bake at 350, it will stand

Patty cake, patty cake

Mommy slide the cake from the oven

Mommy spread the frosting on the layers

Patty cake, patty cake

Mommy slice the cake, and put in a plate

right in my hands.

Patty cake, patty cake, I know mommy can.

Right to the heart

Pink

Pink is a beautiful color to me

In the bright sunshine I see

Never, look down, and frown about pink

you see.

Keep looking around pink is all over town

Pink is a beautiful color to me.

Right to the heart

The boat on the river

The boat on the river

Hearing the whistle blowing

Even blowing during the night

Big and beautiful in the moon light

Oh, I am watching the boat tonight

A little walk on the pier to see the boat near

The stars that are still hanging low

I am walking on the pier to see the boat my

dear.

Right to the heart

Wheels on the wagon

The wheels on the wagon go around and
round.

Go around and round all through the town

Happy little children riding in the wagon

Every wheel on the wagon is just a rolling

Every child is still holding

Laughing and smiling in the wagon, it is

going up and down.

Wheels on the wagon go around, and around

Wagon goes all through the town.

Right to the heart

Walking in the rain

Walking the rain

All day it is still the same

Laugh and smiling it is still the same

Keeping my focus even in the rain

In the midst the rain it is cold and pain

The sky looks beautiful in midst of the rain

Evening will soon appear in the rain

Rainbows appears in the sky God love you

Already you know God is standing by

In the midst just keeping it all real

Never, will I look back, Jesus got me alright.

Right to the heart

Raise Up

Raise up big or small

All raising for a worthy cause

I will never give up nor frown

Safely, you shall keep your feet on the

ground.

Every step you will make today

Until this day Jesus is standing by

Power of God is from on high.

Right to the heart

Love

Love is in the heart

Love is open wide

Love is in the air

Love is very emotional inside

Every day of my life, thank you Jesus for

being my guide.

Right to the heart

Freedom

Freedom is being free

Freedom is being me

Freedom is doing the things I enjoy

Freedom is pressing even the more

Freedom is enjoying life

Freedom is being nice.

Right to the heart

Sweet

Sweet is sweet

Candy is sweet

Sweet is sweet

Cake is sweet

Sweet is sweet

Pie is sweet

Sweet is sweet

Now, they are treats

Sweet is sweet.

Right to the heart

Winter

Winter is winter

Winter is cold

Winter even freezes my noise

Winter even shatter my teeth

Winter even shakes my knees

Winter even make you wear double socks

Winter even make you put on booths to walk

Winter even I put on my coat

Winter even I put on my gloves

Winter even I put on my hat

Winter even, now that is a fact

Winter is winter.

Right to the heart

Break through

Break through your struggles

Releasing your pain

Even now the time is far spent

All the pain you have gained

Keep pushing your way through

The torn heart, and the pain

Hoping someday you will see your way

through.

Reaching again for the rope

Oh, how so much pain

Until dawn break, I will lay awake

God, please come release me from the

heartache.

Your breakthrough has now come, and your

tears have flowed now you done.

Right to the heart

Good morning

Good morning God

Oh, how wonderful it is to be alive

Oh, how beautiful to see another day

Day by day I will always pray

Morning has now arrived

Open your eyes to see the bright sunshine

Rejoicing for another day

Night has now gone away

In the heat of the day

No, need to worry the time has come

Good morning God.

Right to the heart

Flowers

Flowers are beautiful to see

Looking at many different colors

Oh, yes flowers are beautiful to me

Waking up on a beautiful day

Every flower is fresh and colorful to see

Reaching my hands up towards the sky

Sun shinny day, and the flowers are here

to stay.

Right to the heart

Parrots

Parrots are beautiful birds

All different kinds of parrots waiting in line

Right in front of me

Red and green parrots are beautiful to see

Oh, parrots are big and small

Talking to the parrot is fun after all

Singing along with the parrots big and small.

Right to the heart

Sea Gull's over the Ocean

Sea gulls flying over the ocean

Everyday seeing sea gulls flying high

All are beautiful flying in the sky

Gulls are white beautiful creators to see

Upon the wide ocean breeze is a big sea gull

Look, and there is a sea gull watching me

Look you will find all different sizes

Over the beautiful ocean sea gulls flying by

Visiting the beautiful ocean side, and the

bright blue sky.

Every sea shell laying in the sand

Resting on a lovely day, and enjoying the

Sunshine once again.

Every day a beautiful white sea gull flying

by my way, and they play.

Ocean breeze feels good to me

Right to the heart

Calm day to walk any way.

Even in the break of the day

All the sea gulls are flying by my way

Now, a beautiful quite time, and the sea gull

is flying away.

Right to the heart

Thanksgiving

Thanksgiving is a day to give thanks

Happy friends and family giving thanks

All the rushing and shopping for that day

Now, we try to gather, and give God thanks

Keeping all the beautiful smiles on our faces

Singing and giving God all the praises

Giving thanks unto our Lord

It is a blessing to give thanks unto thee

Victory is in the praises, and giving thanks

unto thee.

It is a time to rejoice Oh, Lord in thee

Now, I lift my voice to give thanks unto God

Great is thy name, oh God I give you thanks.

Right to the heart

Mother's Breakfast

Mother's breakfast is smells good to me

Oh, get out of bed you sleep head

Time for breakfast for you to eat

Hurry get dress, and wash your hands

Swiftly making your way to the table

Breakfast is ready don't you see

Ready to break bread once again

Every day God, I thank you for feeding me

Awake now, to bow my head thank Lord for
my daily bread.

Keep thanking you Lord, for my meat and
bread.

Fresh juice ready to drink

All the good breakfast mother had cooked

Sweet smell from to the kitchen just look

Touch of mother's beautiful hands

Mother thank you for the breakfast again.

Right to the heart

Holiday Season

Holiday season is for me

Oh, how happy that day is to me

Laughter and smiles all over town

I love to see the holiday season

Day is so far spent in this season

All around the town the holiday is now

You are baking and decorating

Special season it is to see

Everyday joyful blessing is God indeed

A fresh drop of oil from heaven above

Season is now to rejoice in the Lord

Oh, Lord how I love thee

Now, the holiday season Jesus is the reason.

Right to the heart

Family Time

Family time is important you see

All through the year is spending family time

Making plans cooking, and dinning

I always love spending family time, my dear

Life is full of fun with family you see

You laugh, and shares smile with your

family around you see.

Time is so precious can't you see

In the midst the storm you still hang on

Making every day count for family time

Every tear drops from your eye

Family time is important time, and I love

you now forever.

Right to the heart

A dream

A dream is a dream

Dreams have meaning can't you see

Reaching for the answers to your dream

Every dream there is revelation about the

Situation.

After all your dream is not wasted

My dreams maybe late at night, and that is

alright

A dream is a dream, and that's alright.

Dreams have meaning that's a fact.

Right to the heart

Candy Man

Candy man candy man

Candy man that stood by the bank

Candy man, candy man

All I have is a dollar to buy a snicker bar

Candy man, candy man

Now, how much do you charge

You see the money I have in my hands

Maybe it is a good plan for me

All the different candy I do see

Nice, and neat stacked in a pile

Candy man, candy man, thank you wow.

Right to the heart

Turtle by the tree

The turtle by the tree

The turtle is pretty to me

The turtle by the tree

The turtle is big as can be

The turtle by the tree

The turtle with his head looking at me

The turtle by the tree

The turtle will not move can't you see

The turtle by the tree

The turtle is looking happy, and free

The turtle by the tree.

Right to the heart

Drawing in the sand

Drawing in the sand

I place my finger in the sand

Drawing in the sand

I wonder never to let a day go by

Drawing in the sand

Sating down on the ground

Drawing in the sand

I will never frown

Drawing in the sand

How do I draw in the sand?

Drawing in the sand

Where do I began?

Drawing in the sand

It is like you trying to sketch your way

Drawing in the sand

Look unto Jesus, and he will hold your hand

You will never need to draw again in the

sand. Jesus has all your plans.

Right to the heart

The spoken prayers

The spoken prayers in the night

The spoken prayers and believing God

The spoken prayers in the night

I trust God everything is going to be alright

The spoken prayers in the night

God does hear my prayers

The spoken prayers in the night

God will never hide his from me

The spoken prayers in the night

When, I call on the name of Jesus

The spoken prayers in the night

The name called Jesus, and devil flee

The spoken prayers in the night

Jesus knows how to make everything alright

The spoken prayers in the night.

Right to the heart

Let's give thanks unto God

I will give thanks unto God

Let's, give thanks unto God

The Lord is the one I adore

Let's, give thanks unto God

Even when you are feeling down

Let's, give thanks unto God

Just remember the Lord is always a round

Let's, give thanks unto God

The Lord able to bring sunshine around

Let's, give thanks unto God

The Lord will give you a heavenly glow

Let's, give thanks unto God

You don't have to worry no more

The Lord is standing by your side

Let's, give thanks unto God

The Lord is always good

Let's, give thanks unto God

Let God forever keep you.

Right to the heart

Lord fill my cup

Lord fill my cup

Let it flow with your gentle love

Lord fill my cup

The love that flow from above

Lord fill my cup

The only true love that I adore

Lord fill my cup

Now, I am so thankful unto thee

Lord fill my cup with your love.

Right to the heart

Butterfly

Butterfly in the sky

Butterfly, butterfly

Butterfly is beautiful flying high

Butterfly, butterfly

There is no question, why?

Butterfly, butterfly

Around the flower, and there they go

Butterfly, butterfly

Butterfly may land on the sand

Butterfly, butterfly

Nobody, knows where the butterfly may go

Butterfly, butterfly

The butterfly may even land on your hand

Butterfly, butterfly

Butterfly may land in a flower bed again

Butterfly, butterfly in the sky.

Right to the heart

Florida

Florida is a beautiful place to be

Looking and laughing all in the street

Oh, mine Florida is beautiful to me

Riding up and down the street to see

I see small, big high-rise buildings in the sky

Day and night the lights are flashing bright

All around Florida is a beautiful place just to stay.

Right to the heart

Surprises

Surprises is something wait to see

Up and down surprises are around

Ready to see what it could be

Please don't keep the surprise from me

Ready to see my surprise, yes indeed

I will try to be patient you see

Zip in and out almost about to shout

Every day, I had to sat back and wonder

about what the surprise could be.

Thank you, wow now I see.

Right to the heart

Three little kittens

Three little kittens sating under the tree

Three little kittens looking at me

Happy little kitten sating under the tree

Resting in the shade is where they stay

Every beautiful little kitten now sleeping
today.

Three little kittens are happy and free

Every time, I look around they just meow at
me.

Leaves on the ground from the trees around

Three little kittens laying in the leaves

Three little kittens are beautiful and free.

Right to the heart

Rattle tack, tack

Rattle tack, tack

I hear a cat

Rattle tack, tack

I hear a rat

Rattle, tack, tack

The cat meows

Rattle tack, tack

The rat is in the trap

Rattle tack, tack

The cat hides under a hat.

Right to the heart

The man in the mirror

The man in the mirror

Who can that be?

The man in the mirror

Handsome as he can be

Everything is great can't you see

The man in the mirror

Man is standing tall

Always looking happy, and alone

Nicely dressed, oh wow

In the mirror the man fixes his tie

Not even a frown or a cry

There is a joy just looking in the mirror

Hi, and there is no mistake

Even the man in the mirror got what it takes

Mirror will reflect to you, and it never lie

Right in front of you is a mirror

Man is in the mirror, and no question why?

The man in the mirror is you, that's no lie.

Right to the heart

Singing Praises

Singing praises unto my King

Singing praises unto his Holy name

In the Lord present is love, I will gain

Now the voices of angels are rejoicing

Greeting, and praising God Holy name

In the time of struggle, I will praise his name

Now, the praises of God will go up again

Greatly is the Lord name to be praise

Reaching for the height, I will gain

All the praises in Jesus name

I will sing praise unto my God

Singing praises unto your name, oh God

Every praise, I will sing unto you

Sing praises unto you God.

Right to the heart

North Carolina

Nothing could be better than North Carolina

Oh, waking up is a blessing too

Right in the state, North Carolina a lot to do

There is a blessing being here with you

Happy and smiling everyday too

Carolina is the place for me, and you

All the beautiful flowers, and the trees

Right in the heart of North Carolina you see

Oh, this is the place for me

Life is not a joke

Living in North Carolina is place for hope

In this state the people are fully awake

Never a dull moment in North Carolina

All the things I enjoy, and see North

Carolina is the place to be.

Right to the heart

Christmas

Christmas is a beautiful holiday to see

Happy people and free

Rushing and looking

In a cold misty night

Shopping and to find things alright

Today is a beautiful holiday to me

Making my list and checking it twice

All, the gifts I choice were real nice

Shopping for deals, and now that is for real.

.

Right to the heart

Apple, peaches, pumpkin pie

Apple, peaches, pumpkin pie

Oh, what a good girl am I

Apple, peaches pumpkin pie

Pinched, my finger, and it made me cry

Apple, peaches pumpkin pie

A slice of pie I will love to try

Apple, peaches, pumpkin pie.

Right to the heart

Rain bows in the sky

Rain bow rain bow in the sky

A beautiful promise God made for you, and

I that is a blessing just too see

Rain bow, rain bow in the sky

Beautiful colors before your eyes

Rain bow rain bow in the sky

Yellow, green red and, orange

Rain bow rain bow in the sky

The covenant God had made for us

No more floods on the earth

Rain bow rain bow in the sky

A beautiful promise God made for you, and

I that is a blessing just to see

Rain bow, rain bow in the sky.

Right to the heart

January

January is jacket time yes, we know

All wrapped up tight here we go

Now we are going out the door

Up and ready to go

Alright, just look at the snow

Right in the middle of the cold

You are staying wrapped up to go.

Right to the heart

February

February is a month of love

Every heart is filled with flower, and candy

Bracing to keep the love one you know

Reaching and showing more love to grow

Up in my heart is filled with love

All rejoicing with a glow forever

Ready to open my box of candy

You are always in my heart that's no

Surprise.

Right to the heart

March

March, oh here we go

March is when the wind blow

All the briskly high winds

Rain sometimes creeping in

Chills may run down your spine

Happy to see St. Patrick Day it is on time.

Right to the heart

April

April oh, how well we know

April showers here we go

Rain, rain, want you to go away?

I want to see a dry pretty day

Looking for April to bring beautiful flowers.

Right to the heart

May

May is a good month to stay

May will bring beautiful flowers this way

Already to see what may has in store for me

Yes, May is a beautiful month to see

Right to the heart

June

June, June, June

Now everything has bloom

Up out of bed, no longer is a sleepy head

Now, June is beautiful, and no gloom

Every time, I look around June is a good

season to see things bloom.

Right to the heart

July

July, July, July

July is now before my eyes

July has fireworks in the sky

July has popping sounds all over town

You are happy and free to celebrate the 4th

With me, and watching the fireworks in the

Sky on the 4th July.

Right to the heart

August

August is the month to see

Up at the break of dawn

Getting ready to put my clothes on

Saying a little prayer to start my day

Shower, is the next thing I will do today

August is a great day, and August is still a

hot any way.

Right to the heart

September

September is time for the fall

Even the leaves fall

Praying through the rag weed, and all

Time, now is for the fall

Enjoying seeing the leaves fall

Mine, goodness a fresh look at fall

Bring in the rain, and the leaves change

Enjoying seeing the leaves, and the rain

Resting in my bed because fall is still full
speed ahead.

Right to the heart

October

October is a month of cold breeze

Cold air blowing out right by me

Time to go in the pumpkin patch

Out I will go with my hat

Break time has come, and it's almost nine

Every time I see a big pumpkin it looks fine

Ready to break away from the pumpkin

Patch, and that is a fact.

Right to the heart

November

November is the month for Thanksgiving

Oh, turkey on the table you see

Visiting family is a blessing to me

Every moment is a joyful occasion

Memories of everyone sating around the

Thanksgiving table.

Blessing to see my family that I love so dear

Enjoying Thanksgiving, and knowing God

able.

Resting, enjoying Thanksgiving, and having

a peaceful night.

Right to the heart

December

Deck my home with lots of holly
 Enjoying the season and everybody
Christmas time is in December you see
Every bright eye stirring at me
Making a joyful noise unto my God
Beautiful blessings for ever boy and girl
Every closed eye, and to say good night
Ready to see Christmas morning that's a fact
It is a blessing to see everyone alive, and
well thank you God for your Glory deep
down inside.

Right to the heart

God, I love you

Now, Lord it is another day

Lord I will always continue to pray

As, I fasten my eyes on this beautiful day

The love God, placed in my heart is there to
stay.

Oh, God your nailed scarred hands on
Calvary Cross.

God, you prevented my soul from being lost

God, I thank you for just loving me

God, I love you yes indeed.

.

Right to the heart